FIRST AMERICANS

The Shoshone

SARAH De CAPUA

Marshall Cavendish
Benchmark
New York

ACKNOWLEDGMENTS

Series consultant: Raymond Bial

Marshall Cavendish Benchmark
99 White Plains Road
Tarrytown, New York 10591-9001
www.marshallcavendish.us

Text copyright © 2008 by Marshall Cavendish Corp.
Map and illustrations copyright © 2008 by Marshall Cavendish Corp.
Map and illustrations by Rodica Prato
Craft illustrations by Chris Santoro

Library of Congress Cataloging-in-Publication Data
De Capua, Sarah.
The Shoshone / by Sarah De Capua.
p. cm. — (First Americans)
Summary: "Provides comprehensive information on the background, lifestyle,
beliefs, and present-day lives of the Shoshone people"—Provided by publisher.
Includes bibliographical references and index.
ISBN-13: 978-0-7614-2683-7
1. Shoshone Indians—Juvenile literature. I. Title. II. Series.
E99.S4D4 2007
978.004'974574—dc22
2006034113

Photo research by Connie Gardner
Cover photo by NativeStock, Marilyn "Angel" Wynn
Title page by Corbis, Stapleton Collection, 1.
The photographs in this book are used by permission and through the courtesy of: *Corbis*: Layne Kennedy, 7; Connie Ricci, 11; Richard
Gehmans, 35. *Nativestock*: Marilyn "Angel" Wynn, 4, 13, 16, 18, 20, 24, 26, 28, 30, 33, 38, 39, 41. *NorthWind Picture Archives*: 9.
AP Photo: Wyoming Division of Culture Rescues, 14; Mark Duncan, 36
On the cover: A young girl in traditional clothing enjoys a Shoshone-Bannock festival and powwow.
Title page: This Shoshone hide painting depicts a dance ceremony after a buffalo hunt.

Editor: Deborah Grahame
Publisher: Michelle Bisson
Art Director: Anahid Hamparian
Series designer: Symon Chow

Printed in China
1 3 5 6 4 2

CONTENTS

1 · WHO ARE THE SHOSHONE PEOPLE?

The Shoshone people live on reservations, colonies, or in farming communities in Wyoming, Idaho, and Nevada. They also live on small reservations in Utah and California. Some Shoshone live among their non-Indian neighbors in cities or other parts of the United States. In all, there are about 12,000 Shoshone in the United States.

The Shoshone call themselves by many different names that mean "people." The word *Shoshone* (or *Shoshoni*) may mean "valley dwellers."

Before 1800 the Shoshone lived in the area of the United States known as the Great Basin, in present-day Nevada. This area gets its name because it forms a giant bowl that contains valleys between the Sierra Nevada and the Rocky Mountains. The Great Basin covers an area of about

A Shoshone man and his horse in the Great Basin region

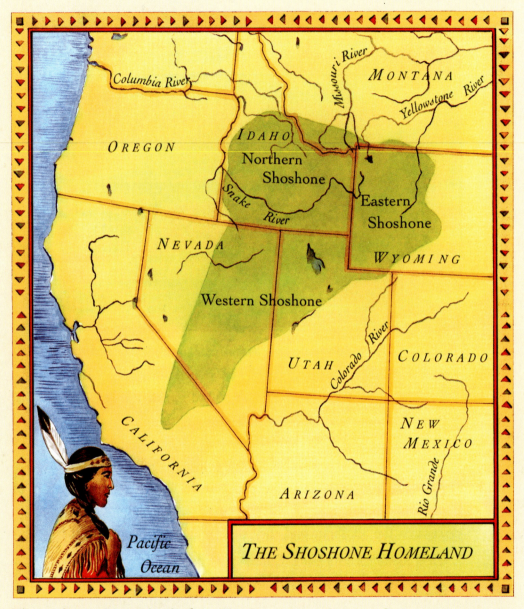

The traditional homeland of the Shoshone covered parts of what are now six U.S. states.

200,000 square miles (518,000 square kilometers). It includes much of the land in what are now the states of Wyoming, Montana, Utah, Nevada, Idaho, and California.

The Shoshone moved seasonally, hunting and gathering food in the Great Basin. Over time, they divided into three groups. The Western Shoshone lived in what are now Utah, Nevada, and California. The Northern Shoshone lived

The Shoshone inhabited this area of present-day Wyoming.

in northern Utah, Idaho, Oregon, and Montana. (A group of Northern Shoshone left the north in the late 1600s. They moved south and became known as the Comanche Indians.) The Eastern Shoshone lived along the Wind River in southwestern Wyoming.

Life in the Great Basin, where some valleys are like deserts, could be hard. Not much rain falls there, so it is difficult to grow crops. But the Great Basin helped protect the Shoshone from outsiders, who did not want to settle in such a harsh environment. As a result, the Shoshone had little contact with non-Indians, except for trappers and fur traders.

In 1803 U.S. president Thomas Jefferson bought land that had previously been owned by France. This land became known as the Louisiana Purchase. For the price of $15 million, 828,000 square miles (2,144,000 sq km) of land were added to the United States, nearly doubling the nation's size. The new territory extended north to south from Canada to the Gulf of Mexico, and east to west from the Mississippi River to the Rocky Mountains. All or part of fifteen U.S. states would be created from the Louisiana Purchase.

The Louisiana Purchase led thousands of settlers to move to the Great Basin. Traveling from the crowded coastal areas of the eastern and southern United States, some settlers passed through the area on their way to Oregon and California. Others remained in the Great Basin permanently.

Among the groups of settlers were the Mormons, who traveled west from Illinois in search of religious freedom. In 1847 they founded Salt Lake City, Utah, in Shoshone territory.

Fur pelts are piled on the boat of these fur traders in Utah.

Sacagawea

After President Jefferson completed the Louisiana Purchase in 1803, he hired Meriwether Lewis and William Clark to explore and map the region. The Lewis and Clark expedition, whose members were called the Corps of Discovery, set out from St. Louis, Missouri, in 1804. They spent the winter in what is now North Dakota, among the Mandan and Hidatsa Indians. There they met a trader named Toussaint Charbonneau, who was living among the Hidatsa with his Shoshone wife Sacagawea ("Bird Woman").

In spring of 1805 Charbonneau, Sacagawea, and their infant son joined the expedition. Sacagawea served as a guide and translator, communicating with the Shoshone, Hidatsa, and other Native Americans the expedition met on the way west to the Pacific Ocean. Sacagawea's presence and ability to explain Lewis and Clark's peaceful mission saved the Corps of Discovery from hostile Indians.

When the expedition ended in 1806, Charbonneau, Sacagawea, and their son returned to live with the Hidatsa. William Clark wrote a note to Charbonneau in which he expressed admiration for the courage and strength of Sacagawea, who had been only about sixteen years old when she joined the Corps of Discovery. Today, Sacagawea is honored as one of the most famous Native American women in history. She appears on the golden U.S. dollar, a coin that went into circulation in 2000.

This sculpture of Sacagawea and her infant son stands in Bismarck, North Dakota.

The Mormons and Shoshone intended to live in peace with each other. But over time, misunderstandings and conflicts led to war.

The discovery of gold in California in 1848, silver in Nevada in 1859, and more gold in Idaho in 1860 led to the arrival of miners who hoped to become rich, and even more settlers. Mining towns sprang up all over Shoshone lands. The addition of so many new people meant there was less **game** for Shoshone hunters. Buffalo became scarce. Settlers cut down piñon trees, whose nuts were a major food source for the Shoshone, to build homes, barns, fences, and corrals. They also took large areas of land for their horses and cattle to graze on.

The Shoshone continued to travel from place to place within the Great Basin, but they found it harder and harder to find the plants and animals they needed for food. Their land was being changed too much for them to survive.

Some Shoshone fought to protect their land and way of

Piñon nuts were an important food source for the Shoshone.

life. They attacked wagon trains, settlers, and railroad and **telegraph** workers. This led to even more conflict between the settlers and the Shoshone. The U.S. government sent the army to protect the settlers. This, too, increased the conflict with the Shoshone, leading to the deaths of many settlers and Shoshone.

After a while, Eastern Shoshone chief Washakie encouraged

Chief Washakie

The exact date of Chief Washakie's birth is unknown, but it was probably in the early 1800s. His name at birth was Pina Quanah ("Smell of Sugar"). Washakie became a noted warrior, leading his people in battle against both the settlers and the Shoshone's Indian enemies, the Sioux and the Cheyenne. By 1850 he was a chief of the Shoshone.

Eventually, Washakie realized it was useless to fight the traders and settlers, so he made friends with them. He aided U.S. Army military operations against Shoshone enemies. He gave the Union Pacific Railroad Company permission to build a portion of the nation's first coast-to-coast railroad on Shoshone lands. Washakie also established the Wind River Reservation in Wyoming, requesting that schools, churches, and hospitals be built on the land. After he died on February 20, 1900, he was buried with full military honors at Wyoming's Fort Washakie, which is named in his honor.

Chief Washakie

his people to make peace with the settlers. He knew that the Shoshone would not be able to drive them away. In 1863 the Northern and Eastern Shoshone signed the First Treaty of Fort Bridger, also called the Five State Treaty. That same year, the Western Shoshone signed the Treaty of Ruby Valley. By signing these treaties, the Shoshone agreed to move onto reservations. In exchange, they received food, medicine, and supplies. The way of life they had known for nearly a thousand years had ended. The Shoshone struggled to adjust to their new life on the reservations. Their struggles continued even after Congress granted U.S. citizenship to all Native Americans in 1924.

Beginning in 1936, however, Congress began to pass laws to improve the lives of the Shoshone and other Native Americans. These laws guaranteed Native Americans the right to practice their tribal customs and speak native languages, gave them a voice in the federal government, and helped them protect their heritage.

2 · LIFE IN THE GREAT BASIN

The **ancestors** of the Shoshone, called the Numic or Shoshonean, were the first people to live in the Great Basin. They moved to the area from the southwest between one thousand and three thousand years ago. There were many different bands of Shoshone. Three of the bands were the *Tipatikka* ("pine nut eaters"), the *Watatikka* ("ryegrass seed eaters"), and the *Akatikka* ("salmon eaters"). All of the Shoshone spoke the same language, but bands that lived in different areas had their own ways of life, including their own unique beliefs and customs.

The harsh, dry climate of the Great Basin forced the Shoshone to **adapt** in order to survive. They used branches and grasses to build summer shelters called wickiups. Wickiups were easy to make. They were built with three

Bands of Shoshone gather in the Great Basin.

wooden poles covered with dried grass. In winter the Shoshone lived in caves or wickiups covered in elk hides. The Northern Shoshone lived in cone-shaped huts during winter. These huts were made of poles tied together with bark, grass, or brush, and supported by a ring of stones. (After making contact with Plains Indians, many Northern and Eastern Shoshone began to live in tepees.)

A Northern Shoshone family pose beside their winter dwelling.

The Shoshone also adapted to the Great Basin's environment by keeping the size of their family groups to between twenty and thirty people. They did this because food and water were scarce. There was not enough for too many people at one time. A band was made up of the members of two to ten families. Most bands had a chief, or principal leader, who made important decisions. Bands without a chief turned to their oldest and wisest members for leadership.

Shoshone families were made up of a man, a woman, and their children. Several families lived together, and every family member had specific jobs to do. Men hunted, fished, protected their families, and served as leaders. Women gathered food, and cared for the camp and the children.

Shoshone men made weapons and arrowheads out of animal bone. They also made bows and arrows, spears, and fishing nets. Men hunted alone or in small groups. They hunted elk, bighorn sheep, mule deer, and pronghorns (a relative of the antelope). Some Eastern and Northern

Shoshone hunted buffalo. Birds, rabbits, and fish, especially salmon, were also common sources of food.

Shoshone women preserved and cooked the game and fish that the men brought back to camp. Women also prepared animal hides for clothing and blankets. They put up the shelters and took them down, and gathered nuts from piñon trees, as well as seeds, roots, berries, and leaves. They also gathered plants that were used as medicine, and wove baskets that were used to carry everything from berries to water.

Children learned the Shoshone way of life by watching and helping adults. Shoshone children did not go to school. Boys hunted and fished with their fathers, while girls helped their mothers. Both boys and girls collected bird eggs for food, and helped the men hunt rabbits by chasing the animals toward the hunters' nets.

The Shoshone did not believe in physical punishment. They believed that hitting a child would harm his or her spirit. When children misbehaved, adults told them that

The root of the camas, or lily, plant was boiled or roasted and then added to stew.

they were disappointed and ashamed of the poor behavior. This was usually enough to make children behave properly.

During the hot summers, the Shoshone wore little clothing. Women wore aprons made of woven plants or the hide of mule deer or pronghorns. Men dressed in **breechcloths** made of mule deer or pronghorn hide.

Shoshone Craft: Leather Pouch

The Shoshone kept herbs and other plants in animal-skin pouches. They used these herbs and plants as medicines. The pouches also held personal items. You can make your own leather pouch to wear around your neck.

You will need:

- 2 pieces of leather, each measuring about 3 inches by 4 inches (8 centimeters by 10 centimeters) (You can buy leather at craft or hobby stores.)
- a piece of yarn in any color, about 3 feet (1 meter) long
- tracing paper
- pencil
- scissors
- hammer and awl
- a block of wood to work on
- newspaper to protect your work area
- an adult helper
- a large bead, to hold the pouch closed
- feathers, beads, markers, or paint and paintbrushes, to decorate your pouch

1· Spread out the newspaper on a large, flat surface to cover and protect your work area.

2· Trace a pouch pattern like the one shown in the illustration (right) onto the tracing paper. Then cut out the pattern.

3· Place the pattern on top of one piece of leather and cut the leather into the pouch shape. Repeat this step with the second piece of leather.

4· Put the two pieces of leather side by side, with the right sides facing out.

5· Place the block of wood in front of you. Put the leather pieces on top of it. Ask your adult helper to guide you as you use the hammer and awl to make holes about $1/2$ inch (1 centimeter) apart along the edge of the two layers of leather.

6· "Sew" the yarn through the holes, pushing it into each hole with your finger and then pulling it through. You can use an in-and-out (running) stitch or a looping (blanket) stitch (see the illustrations at right). Do this until you have sewn all the way around the pouch.

7· Pull the yarn through until the ends are even. Push the bead over the ends of the yarn and slide it down to close the pouch.

8· Tie the ends of the yarn in a knot and slip it over your head so your pouch is worn like a long necklace. You may want to glue feathers or beads to your pouch, or draw or paint pictures on it.

Wear your pouch and share what you have learned about the Shoshone with others!

Shoshone moccasins decorated with beadwork

During winter, men and women wore robes or leggings made of animal fur. After the arrival of the Europeans in the 1500s, the Shoshone wore clothing made of wool or leather in winter. Children wore smaller versions of adults' clothing. The Shoshone usually went barefoot, but they did wear moccasins during cold weather, on journeys, and in areas where the ground was rough.

Depending on where they lived, Shoshone women wore their hair long with a part down the middle and a braid on each side of the head. Men also wore their hair long. After they began to trade with other tribes, some Shoshone warriors began to wear headdresses made of eagle, red-tailed hawk, magpie, or swan feathers.

Recipe: Piñon Brittle

When preparing this recipe, be sure you do not confuse piñon nuts (sometimes called "real piñon") with Nevada pine nuts. They have very different tastes. Ask an adult to help you make this recipe, which comes from the recipe section of Piñon Nuts (www.pinonnuts.com), a source for mail-order piñon nuts. You can also buy piñon nuts at health food stores. Always wash your hands with soap and water before you begin.

- 1 cup piñon nuts, shelled
- $1/2$ teaspoon salt
- 2 cups granulated sugar

Melt the sugar over low heat, stirring constantly until it becomes a thin syrup. Stir in the piñon nuts and salt, and pour out the mixture onto a large buttered cookie sheet. (The mixture will form a thin layer on the cookie sheet.) Put the cookie sheet in the refrigerator and allow the mixture to cool overnight. Once the candy is cold and hard, break it into pieces and enjoy!

3 · SHOSHONE BELIEFS

The Shoshone believed that respecting and honoring the spirit world would bring good luck. They believed Wolf created the world and Coyote created the people. Wolf was called "Creator," or *Appáh* ("Our Father"). Coyote, or *Ishapah*, was called "Our Father's Brother." Two other important spirits were Bear ("Our Father's Sister") and Rattlesnake ("Our Father's Father"). The Shoshone called the earth "Mother."

The Shoshone believed that spirits lived in the land, rivers, mountains, and plants—especially in sagebrush and piñon trees. Spirits also lived in the sun, moon, and stars. The spirits had powers that could help or hurt the Shoshone. In order to receive the spirits' help, the Shoshone performed **rituals** to please them. Rituals to give thanks to the spirits followed births, marriages, and deaths. Shoshone

An Eastern Shoshone woman prays to the spirits of nature.

A Shoshone hunter covered with a deer hide performs a dance meant to bring a successful deer hunt.

hunters and warriors prayed to the spirits for success in the hunt and in battle.

Dancing was a big part of Shoshone rituals. Common dances included the Chokecherry Dance, the Ghost Dance, the Round Dance, the War Dance, and the Warm Dance. Some of the dances took several days to perform.

Each dance had its own meaning. Some dances were

prayers for abundant piñon nuts, roots, and berries to collect as food. Others were prayers for a successful hunt, for safety, or for victory over evil spirits, which were believed to cause illness. Still other dances were performed to give thanks or to celebrate the life of a person who had died. Many of these traditional dances are still performed today.

People who were believed to possess special powers were called shamans. A shaman was a holy person who used spiritual powers to see the unknown, control events, or heal the sick. Shamans received their power during a vision quest. Vision quests were rites of passage in which Native American youths went off alone to seek guidance from the spirits through fasting and prayer. Shamans who healed illness were called "medicine men" or "medicine women" by non-Indians, but the Shoshone called them *puhagan* or *puha*.

The Shoshone usually chose their own spouses, but sometimes parents arranged marriages for their children. Most men had only one wife at a time, but if there were more women than men in a band, a Shoshone man might have two or three wives. Likewise, if men outnumbered women, a woman might have more than one husband. The Shoshone did not have wedding ceremonies. The couple simply moved in together. For the first year of marriage, the couple usually lived with the wife's family. After the husband proved that he could provide for his wife, the couple moved into their own home.

When a Shoshone couple was expecting a child, they followed a set of rituals that were thought to ensure that the baby would be healthy. The couple, particularly the mother, followed a strict diet

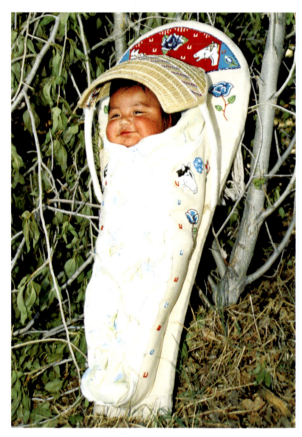

Shoshone babies were strapped onto frames called cradleboards so they could be carried easily on their mothers' backs.

and drank hot water, which was believed to make labor easier. The father bathed and fasted. Shoshone women gave birth in special lodges, with help from a **midwife**. The newborn baby was washed in clean, warm water. The mother and child lived apart from the rest of the camp for a month. After they completed a ritual that was meant to purify them, they returned to the camp.

Even though children had chores to do, they had plenty of time to play games. A favorite game was one in which they rolled a hoop made of willow branches over the ground, guiding it with a stick. Girls enjoyed string games, including one that has come to be known as cat's cradle. This game prepared girls for the job of weaving baskets. Boys held archery contests, which helped them learn to hunt. All children and adults enjoyed the hand game.

When a Shoshone died, the other members of the band painted the body with red and white stripes. They then buried the body with items that the person had valued in life.

Hand Game

The hand game was also known as the bone or stick game or, after contact with Europeans, the bullet or button game. Players were divided into two teams. Each team lined up facing the other. While the players sang or beat a rhythm on a drum, the players on one team passed two small bones, bullets, buttons, or other objects from team member to team member. Players on the passing team would make many gestures and talk loudly to try to distract the opposing team. When the song ended or the drum beats stopped, the opponents had to guess which players were holding the objects. If the opponents guessed correctly, they received one of the objects (there were ten in all) and it was their turn to pass the items. The team that guessed incorrectly had to turn over one of its objects for every incorrect guess. Once all the objects were located, the teams reversed roles. The game continued this way until one team held all the objects.

Materials, including sticks and a drum, that were used in the hand game

For a man, these items might be weapons, such as a favorite bow. For a woman, they might be baskets she had woven. The grave was covered with large stones to protect it from wild animals. The band mourned for two days. During this time, the people burned sagebrush to help the dead person's spirit move on to the next world, where it would find peace and wealth. The burning sagebrush was also intended to protect the living from evil spirits.

The dead person's family mourned for one year. Women and men might use knives to cut their legs. Women sometimes blackened their faces or bodies with tar. They also cut their hair very short. Men cut their long hair to shoulder length. People of both genders wore the same clothes every day for the entire mourning period.

When the year of mourning was over, family members painted themselves red and put on new clothes. The other members of the community joined them in a Round Dance, which marked the end of their mourning.

How the Shoshone Came to Be

One of the Shoshone's creation stories says that Coyote left the Great Basin and took a long journey to the place where the sun rose. There he found a wife. Together they had many children, which became all of the Indian tribes. Coyote placed all his children in a basket and went back to the Great Basin. He kept opening the basket as he traveled, and most of the children fell out all over North America. When he reached the Great Basin, the only two tribes left in the basket were the Shoshone and the Paiute. At first these two tribes fought, but Coyote told them they must not fight because they were the only children he had left, and they were the best of his children.

4 · A CHANGING WORLD

During the late 1800s and early 1900s, the U.S. government took back many of the Shoshone's reservation lands. In 1934, however, Congress passed the Indian Reorganization Act. This was a plan to improve the economy and lives of Native Americans throughout the United States. The law gave Native American tribes the right to govern themselves. It also gave some land back to the Native Americans, and encouraged them to preserve their culture by passing it on to their children.

Today, there are ten reservations, four colonies, and five farming communities called *rancherias* where many Shoshone live. These places are located in Wyoming, Idaho, Utah, Nevada, and California. The Shoshone share some lands

This grandmother (left), daughter, and granddaughter are related to Sacagawea's brother. They are an example of the way in which the Shoshone proudly pass along their heritage to family members.

with the Arapaho, Bannock, Goshute, Paiute, and Washoe Indian nations. Some Shoshone also live in cities and towns all over the United States.

Members of the Shoshone tribe still practice many of their traditional ways. They maintain their language, beliefs, and unique identity as Native Americans. At the same time, they live in the modern world.

After Native Americans were granted the right to govern themselves, the Shoshone organized their bands into tribal councils. Each council is made up of a chairperson and five other members who are elected by the band. The councils make decisions about education, employment, health care, and the economy. Business councils make

This present-day Shoshone family lives in Nevada.

decisions on issues such as drilling for oil and natural gas, and the mining of uranium that take place on Shoshone lands.

Many Northern Shoshone went to live with the Bannock Indians on the Fort Hall Indian Reservation in Idaho. The tribes have merged and are now known as the Shoshone-Bannock. Their land is good for farming. They grow crops that include potatoes, wheat, and alfalfa. They also run successful businesses, such as stores, restaurants, and a casino.

The Eastern Shoshone live beside the Rocky Mountains on the Wind River Reservation in Wyoming, which they share

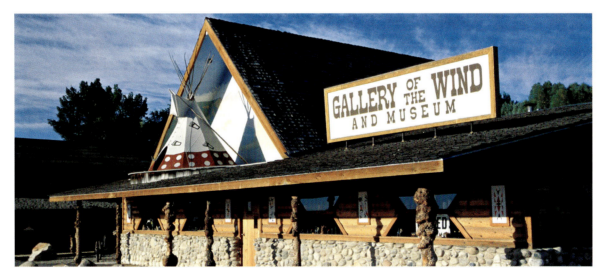

The Shoshone run many successful businesses. This one is located in Wyoming.

with the Arapaho. The land there is not good for farming, so tribe members raise cattle, buffalo, and horses instead. They allow non-Indian farmers to graze livestock on their land for a fee. Many tribe members work for the National Park Service as tour guides, food vendors, or shop clerks, assisting the tourists who visit Yellowstone and Grand Teton national parks. Some Shoshone also work as wilderness guides for visitors who want to go camping, hiking, trail riding, or fishing.

The Western Shoshone have joined with the Paiute and have become known as the Shoshone-Paiute. Their Duck Valley Reservation straddles the state line between Idaho and Nevada. The Shoshone have become successful sheep, horse, and cattle ranchers. Tourism and managing several **hydroelectric** projects are other ways they make a living. Like other Native American nations who receive money from the U.S. government, the Western Shoshone use the funds to support educational, housing, and economic activities that will ensure their future independence.

All Shoshone, wherever they live, attend schools. Many go on to college and become doctors, businesspeople, artists, and engineers, or work in other professions. They stay informed about tribal issues through the Internet and tribal newspapers and magazines.

Every year in August, the Shoshone-Bannock Indian Festival takes place in Idaho. Traditional songs and dances are performed, and tribal arts and crafts are displayed. During Shoshone Days, on the Wind River Reservation in Wyoming, rodeos, powwows, races, and parades are held to celebrate Shoshone heritage. These and other gatherings offer the Shoshone a chance to keep in touch with their rich history.

A Shoshone festival powwow

· TIME LINE

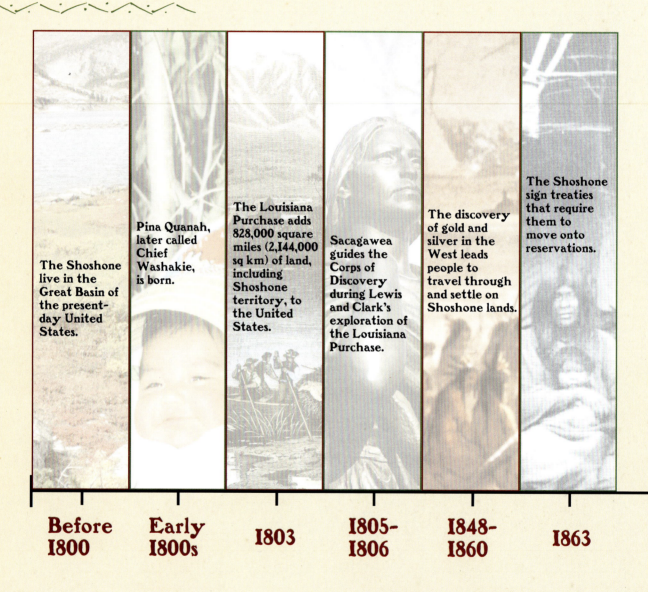

The Shoshone live in the Great Basin of the present-day United States.

Pina Quanah, later called Chief Washakie, is born.

The Louisiana Purchase adds 828,000 square miles (2,144,000 sq km) of land, including Shoshone territory, to the United States.

Sacagawea guides the Corps of Discovery during Lewis and Clark's exploration of the Louisiana Purchase.

The discovery of gold and silver in the West leads people to travel through and settle on Shoshone lands.

The Shoshone sign treaties that require them to move onto reservations.

Before 1800 **Early 1800s** **1803** **1805–1806** **1848–1860** **1863**

Chief Washakie dies.

Congress passes the Indian Citizenship Act, making all Native Americans U.S. citizens.

Congress passes the Indian Reorganization Act, a series of laws designed to improve life for the Shoshone and other Native Americans. It guaranteed Native American tribes the right to govern themselves.

The Shoshone organize their bands into tribal councils.

The golden U.S. dollar, bearing the likeness of Sacagawea, goes into circulation.

1900   **1924**   **1934**   **1938**   **2000**

GLOSSARY

adapt: To make changes in order to survive in a particular environment.

ancestors: Family members who lived a long time ago.

breechcloths: Simple garments worn by men that extend from the waist to the upper thigh.

game: Wild animals, including birds, that are hunted for food or sport.

hydroelectric: Having to do with the production of electricity by means of water power that is used to turn a generator.

midwife: A woman who is specially trained to assist in childbirth.

rituals: Actions that are always performed in the same way as part of a religious ceremony or social custom.

telegraph: A device or system for sending messages over long distances. It uses a code of electric signals sent by wire or radio.

FIND OUT MORE

Books

Erdrich, Liselotte. *Sacagawea*. Minneapolis: Carolrhoda Books, 2003.

Gray-Kanatiiosh, Barbara A. *Shoshone*. Edina, MN: ABDO Publishing, 2004.

Ryan, Marla Felkins. *Shoshone*. San Diego: Blackbirch Press, 2003.

Santella, Andrew. *Lewis and Clark*. Danbury, CT: Franklin Watts, 2002.

Web Sites

www.easternshoshone.net

This is the official Web site of the Eastern Shoshone tribe. It includes information about the Eastern Shoshone's history and culture, as well as facts about the Wind River Reservation in Wyoming.

www.shoshonebannocktribes.com

This is the official Web site of the Shoshone-Bannock tribes. Here you will find the history of the tribes, current tribal news, and descriptions and photos from the Shoshone-Bannock Festival.

www.shoshonidictionary.com

Here you will find a Shoshone-English dictionary and links to other sites on Shoshone language, history, and culture.

About the Author

Sarah De Capua is the author of many books, including biographies and geographical and historical titles. She has always been fascinated by the earliest inhabitants of North America. In the First Americans series, De Capua has also written *The Cherokee*, *The Cheyenne*, *The Comanche*, *The Iroquois*, and *The Shawnee.* Born and raised in Connecticut, she now resides in Colorado.

INDEX

Page numbers in **boldface** are illustrations.